Beginning Serverless Architectures with Microsoft Azure

I0020383

Design scalable applications and microservices that effortlessly adapt to the requirements of your customers

Daniel Bass

BIRMINGHAM - MUMBAI

Beginning Serverless Architectures with Microsoft Azure

Acquisitions Editor: Aditya Date
Content Development Editors: Darren Patel, Tanmayee Patil
Production Coordinator: Ratan Pote

First published: July 2018

Production reference: 1250718

Published by Packt Publishing Ltd.
Livery Place
35 Livery Street
Birmingham
B3 2PB, UK.

ISBN 978-1-78953-704-8

www.packtpub.com

`mapt.io`

Mapt is an online digital library that gives you full access to over 5,000 books and videos, as well as industry leading tools to help you plan your personal development and advance your career. For more information, please visit our website.

Why Subscribe?

- Spend less time learning and more time coding with practical eBooks and Videos from over 4,000 industry professionals
- Improve your learning with Skill Plans built especially for you
- Get a free eBook or video every month
- Mapt is fully searchable
- Copy and paste, print, and bookmark content

PacktPub.com

Did you know that Packt offers eBook versions of every book published, with PDF and ePub files available? You can upgrade to the eBook version at `www.PacktPub.com` and as a print book customer, you are entitled to a discount on the eBook copy. Get in touch with us at `service@packtpub.com` for more details.

At `www.PacktPub.com`, you can also read a collection of free technical articles, sign up for a range of free newsletters, and receive exclusive discounts and offers on Packt books and eBooks.

Contributors

About the Author

Daniel Bass studied Masters of Physics at University College London before becoming a developer at a large financial company. He's part of a team that develops complex backend systems entirely on Azure, making heavy use of event-driven Azure Functions and Azure Data Lake. He's currently working with Azure Web Apps, Sitecore CMS and Build and Release Automation using Visual Studio Team Services.

About the Reviewer

Chantel Spencer-Bowdage likes to break problems apart and build solutions. She is currently working as a full stack software developer with Memrise. She is also a technology director with Girls in Tech, London. She gained experience working with companies such as M&G Investments and MWR InfoSecurity. She completed her Master of Engineering from the University of Southampton. Chantel enjoys a range of hobbies, from drawing to learning Spanish. She also likes travelling to new places. You can find out more about Chantel on her LinkedIn profile: *chantelsb*.

Packt is Searching for Authors Like You

If you're interested in becoming an author for Packt, please visit `authors.packtpub.com` and apply today. We have worked with thousands of developers and tech professionals, just like you, to help them share their insight with the global tech community. You can make a general application, apply for a specific hot topic that we are recruiting an author for, or submit your own idea.

Table of Contents

Preface

Many businesses are rapidly adopting a microservices-first approach to development, driven by the availability of new commercial services like Azure Functions and AWS Lambda. In this book, we'll show you how to quickly get up and running with your own serverless development on Microsoft Azure. We start by working through a single function, and work towards integration with other Azure services like App Insights and Cosmos DB to handle common user requirements like analytics and highly performant distributed storage. We finish up by providing you with the context you need to get started on a larger project of your own choosing, leaving you equipped with everything you need to migrate to a cloud-first serverless solution.

After completing this book, you will be able to:

- Identify the key advantages and disadvantages of serverless development
- Build a fully-functioning serverless application and utilize a wide variety of Azure services
- Create, deploy and manage your own Azure Functions in the cloud
- Implement core design principles for writing effective serverless code

Who This Book Is For

This book is ideal for backend developers or engineers who want a quick hands-on introduction to developing serverless applications within the Microsoft ecosystem.

What This Book Covers

Chapter 1, *Introduction to Azure Functions*, will walk you through the basic understanding of Azure Functions and then its serverless functionalities. In this chapter, we will learn to create, debug, and deploy the Azure Functions. Later in the chapter, we'll deal with serverless runtime functions of Microsoft's Azure Function.

Chapter 2, *Deploying Azure Serverless*, will help you to integrate your Azure Function with Cosmos DB, and with an Azure App Service. Later in the chapter, we'll use APIs to secure the Azure Functions and using Azure Application Insights we'll combine a complete logging and monitoring solution.

`Chapter 3`, *Architecting Serverless Solutions*, will be dealing with triggering functions with Cosmos DB and changing the functionality from an old .NET app to an Azure Function. We'll be developing a weather-dependent notification for our personal finance app. Later in the chapter, we'll analyze how to integrate old applications using serverless architecture.

To Get the Most out of This Book

You should have a basic knowledge of C# and a general knowledge of Azure. Knowledge of ASP.NET/MVC is beneficial but is not mandatory. The minimum hardware requirements are: Intel Core i3 or equivalent, 4GB RAM, 10 GB hard disk, and a stable internet connection. You'll also need the following software installed in advance:

- Google Chrome or Mozilla Firefox (Latest updates installed)
- Postman app for API Development Environment
- Visual Studio 2017 with Azure Development Workflow (Latest version)
- Node.js with Azure-functions-core-tools version 1.x installed via npm
- .NET Framework 4.6 or higher

Download the Example Code Files

You can download the example code files for this book from your account at `www.packtpub.com`. If you purchased this book elsewhere, you can visit `www.packtpub.com/support` and register to have the files emailed directly to you.

You can download the code files by following these steps:

1. Log in or register at `www.packtpub.com`.
2. Select the **SUPPORT** tab.
3. Click on **Code Downloads & Errata**.
4. Enter the name of the book in the **Search** box and follow the onscreen instructions.

Once the file is downloaded, please make sure that you unzip or extract the folder using the latest version of:

- WinRAR/7-Zip for Windows
- Zipeg/iZip/UnRarX for Mac
- 7-Zip/PeaZip for Linux

The code bundle for the book is also hosted on GitHub at `https://github.com/TrainingByPackt/Beginning-Serverless-Architectures-with-Microsoft-Azure`. In case there's an update to the code, it will be updated on the existing GitHub repository.

We also have other code bundles from our rich catalog of books and videos available at `https://github.com/PacktPublishing/`. Check them out!

Conventions Used

There are a number of text conventions used throughout this book.

`CodeInText`: Indicates code words in text, database table names, folder names, filenames, file extensions, pathnames, dummy URLs, user input, and Twitter handles. Here is an example: "The example is called `BeginningAzureServerlessArchitecture`, so all code snippets will refer to that namespace."

A block of code is set as follows:

```
{
  Amount: 47.32,
  ExecutionTime: "2018-01-01T09:00:00Z"
}
```

When we wish to draw your attention to a particular part of a code block, the relevant lines or items are set in bold:

```
class Transaction
  {
    public DateTime ExecutionTime { get; set; }
    public Decimal Amount { get; set; }
  }
```

Bold: Indicates a new term, an important word, or words that you see onscreen. For example, words in menus or dialog boxes appear in the text like this. Here is an example: "Right-click on your project and select **Publish**. Select **Create New Azure Function App**."

Activity: These are scenario-based activities that will let you practically apply what you've learned over the course of a complete section. They are typically in the context of a real-world problem or situation.

 Warnings or important notes appear like this.

Get in Touch

Feedback from our readers is always welcome.

General feedback: Email feedback@packtpub.com and mention the book title in the subject of your message. If you have questions about any aspect of this book, please email us at questions@packtpub.com.

Errata: Although we have taken every care to ensure the accuracy of our content, mistakes do happen. If you have found a mistake in this book, we would be grateful if you would report this to us. Please visit www.packtpub.com/submit-errata, selecting your book, clicking on the Errata Submission Form link, and entering the details.

Piracy: If you come across any illegal copies of our works in any form on the Internet, we would be grateful if you would provide us with the location address or website name. Please contact us at copyright@packtpub.com with a link to the material.

If you are interested in becoming an author: If there is a topic that you have expertise in and you are interested in either writing or contributing to a book, please visit authors.packtpub.com.

Reviews

Please leave a review. Once you have read and used this book, why not leave a review on the site that you purchased it from? Potential readers can then see and use your unbiased opinion to make purchase decisions, we at Packt can understand what you think about our products, and our authors can see your feedback on their book. Thank you!

For more information about Packt, please visit packtpub.com.

Introduction to Azure Functions

1

Serverless programming has been a buzzword in technology for a while now, first implemented for arbitrary code by Amazon on **Amazon Web Services** (**AWS**) in 2014, and first spoken about two years before that. The term normally refers to snippets of backend code running in environments that are wholly managed by the cloud provider, totally invisible to developers. This approach has some astounding benefits, enabling an entirely new paradigm of computing architecture. Now, let's understand the benefits and drawbacks of serverless computing.

Following are the benefits of serverless computing:

- Speed of development
- Zero management (near)
- Cost/cost flexibility
- Auto-scaling

Following are the drawbacks of serverless computing:

- Warmup latency
- Vendor lock-in
- Lack of control for specific use cases

Serverless code can be scaled to handle as much demand as your cloud provider's data center can handle—it is essentially infinite for all but the most demanding applications. However, the real key is elastic, unmanaged scaling. Rather than having to manually set the scale at which your code is running (for example, by spinning up extra virtual machines), serverless code will react to the demand, and scale appropriately. This means that you are charged according to computing resource usage, rather than paying in advance for a scale that you might need for an expected spike of users. It also means that serverless code needs no active management whatsoever—only monitoring. This has some profound impacts, and leads to an architecture that tends toward the microservices approach.

We will introduce this new architecture from the bottom up, starting by creating serverless code, and then building a serverless application. Our first objective will be to create a simple RESTful API with serverless code, before venturing into more interesting and unusual architectures that are unique to serverless code. This book will focus on Microsoft's serverless product Azure Functions.

By the end of this chapter, you will be able to:

- Identify the benefits and drawbacks of serverless computing
- Create an Azure Function
- Debug an Azure Function locally
- Deploy an Azure Function
- Explain the Azure Functions runtime

Understanding the Real Benefits of Serverless Computing

While serverless computing has a compelling set of benefits, it is no silver bullet. To architect effective solutions, you need to be aware of its strengths and weaknesses, which are shown in the following table:

Benefits	Drawbacks
Speed of development	Warmup latency
Automatic scaling	Vendor lock-in
Flexible costs	Lack of low-level control
Little active management	

Benefits

We will discuss each of its main benefits in detail here.

Speed of Development

Firstly, a major strength of serverless computing is its speed of development. The developer doesn't have to concern oneself with, or write any of the code for, the underlying architecture. The process of listening for HTTP messages (or other data inputs/events) and routing is done entirely by the cloud provider, with only some configuration provided by the developer. This allows a developer to simply write code that implements business logic, and deploy it straight to Azure. Each function can then be tested independently.

Automatic Scaling

Secondly, serverless computing has automatic scaling by default. The routing system in a serverless service like Azure Functions will detect how many requests are coming in and deploy the serverless code to more servers when necessary. It will also reduce the number of servers all the way down to zero, if necessary. This is particularly useful if you are running an advertisement or a publicity stunt of some kind—half-time advertisements in the Premier League final, for example. Your backend can instantly scale to handle the massive influx of new users for this brief period of time, before returning to normal very quickly. It's also useful for separating out what would usually be a large, monolithic backend. Some of the parts of the backend will probably be used a lot more than others, but usually, you have to scale the whole thing manually to keep the most-utilized functions responsive. If each function is separated, automatically scaling it allows the developer to identify and optimize the most-used functions.

Flexible Costs

Continuing on the subject of being able to scale down to zero servers, the cost of serverless code is very flexible. Due to auto-scaling, providers are able to charge according to resource usage. This means that you only pay according to usage, which has benefits for all developers, but for small businesses most of all. If your business has lots of customers one month, you can scale accordingly and pay your higher bill with the higher revenue you have made. If you have a quieter month, your serverless computing bill will be proportionally lower for that lower revenue period.

Reduced Management Overhead

Finally, serverless code requires very little active management. An application running on a shared server will usually require a significant amount of monitoring and management, for both the server itself and its resource allocation at any given moment. Containerized code, or code running on virtual machines, is better, but still requires either container management software or a person to monitor the usage and then scale down or scale up appropriately, even if the server itself no longer requires active management. Serverless code has no server visible to the developer and will scale according to demand, meaning that it requires monitoring only for exceptions or security issues, with no real active management to keep a normal service running.

Drawbacks

Serverless code does have some weaknesses which are described here.

Warmup Latency

The first weakness is warmup latency. Although the traffic managers of various platforms (AWS, Azure, Google Cloud, and so on) are very good at responding to demand when there are already instances of serverless code running, it's a very different problem when there are no instances running at all. The traffic managers need to detect the message, allocate a server, and deploy the code to it before running it. This is necessarily slower than having a constantly running container or server. One way to combat this is to keep your code small and simple, as the biggest slowdown in this process can be transferring large code files.

Vendor Lock-in

Secondly, there is the issue of vendor lock-in. Each cloud provider implements its serverless service differently, so serverless code written for Azure is difficult to port over to AWS. If prices spike heavily in the future, then you will be locked in to that provider for your serverless architecture.

There's also the issue of languages. JavaScript is the only language that is universally available, with patchy service across providers for other languages, like C# and Java. There is a solution to this, however; it is called the **serverless framework**. This is a framework that you can use to write simple HTTP-triggered functions, which can then be deployed to all of the major cloud providers. Unfortunately, this means that you will miss out on a lot of the best features of Azure Functions, because their real power comes from deep integration with other Azure services.

Lack of Low-Level Control

Finally, there is the issue of a lack of low-level control. If you are writing a low latency trading platform, then you may be used to accessing networking ports directly, manually allocating memory, and executing some commands using processor-specific code. Your own application might require similar low-level access, and this isn't possible in serverless computing. One thing to bear in mind, however, is that it's possible to have part of the application running on a server that you have low-level access to, and background parts of it running in a serverless function.

If an Azure Function isn't executed for a while, the function stops being deployed and the server gets reallocated to other work. When the next request comes in the function needs to deploy the code, warm up the server and execute the code, so it's slower. Inevitably, this leads to latency when the functions are triggered again, making serverless computing somewhat unsuitable for use cases that demand continuous low-latency. Also, by its very nature, serverless computing prevents you from accessing low level commands and the performance benefits that they can give. It's important to emphasize that this doesn't mean serverless computing is unbearably slow; it just means that applications that demand the utmost performance are unlikely to be suitable for serverless computing.

Overall, there is a clear benefit to using serverless computing, and particularly, Azure Serverless, especially if you use some of the tips detailed in the weaknesses section. The benefits are strong for both the developer and the business.

The serverless framework (`https://serverless.com/`) can help with vendor lock-in by making your serverless functions cross-cloud.

Creating, Debugging, and Deploying an Azure Function

In this section, we will create an Azure Function in Visual Studio, debug it locally, and deploy it to an Azure cloud instance. While doing this, we will cover material about the basics of serverless runtime and the high-level benefits and disadvantages of serverless computing.

The core of all serverless products is to get straight into development with minimal setup time, so that's what we'll do in this subtopic. You should have a serverless function in the cloud at the end of this topic, and once you've learned the ropes, you could create and deploy one in a few minutes.

 To develop Azure Functions for production, you need a computer running Windows and Visual Studio 2015 or later; however, the smoothest experience is present on Visual Studio 2017, version 15.4 or later. If your computer can run Visual Studio, it can handle Azure Function development.

An Azure Function can be written in several languages. At the time of writing, there are three languages with full support: C#, JavaScript, and F#. Generally, the most popular languages are C# and JavaScript. Java is a language in preview, but, being in preview, it is not ready for production yet, so it will not be covered.

 There are also lots of other languages available experimentally for Azure Function runtime version 1 (Python, PowerShell, and so on), but it is not advised to use these for your business architecture, and they will generally fall behind the curve for new features and support. There is also a version 2 of the runtime, but this is only in preview at the time of writing, and is therefore not ready for production.

It's interesting to note that Azure Data Lake and Azure Data Lake Analytics could be considered serverless programming, too. These are designed for processing very large datasets using a new language, U-SQL. You can read about them at https://docs.microsoft.com/en-us/azure/data-lake-analytics/data-lake-analytics-overview.

Visual Studio 2017 has a comprehensive suite of Azure tools, including Azure Function development. While it's possible to use a combination of any other IDE and the command-line interface to develop Azure Functions, the best tooling will always arrive on Visual Studio first.

Creating Your First Function to Receive and Process Data from an HTTP Request

Before you begin, confirm that you have Visual Studio 2017 version 15.4 installed; if not, download and install it. To do so, perform the following steps:

1. Open the **Visual Studio Installer**, which will show you the version of Visual Studio that you have installed and allow you to select the Azure Workflow and install it, if it is missing, then update Visual Studio, if required, to latest version:

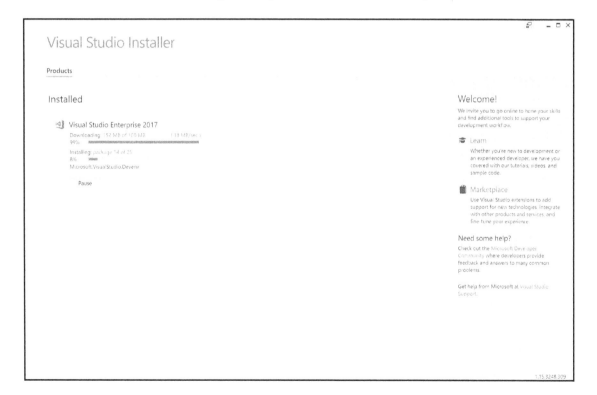

2. Click on **Modify**, select the **Azure development** workload, and click on **Modify** again:

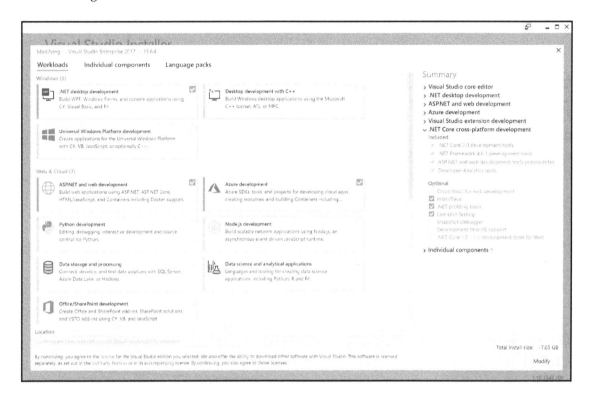

Refer to the complete code placed at `Code/Serverless-Architectures-with-Azure/Lesson1/BeginningAzureServerlessArchitecture/BeginningAzureServerlessArchitecture.csproj`.

Go to `https://goo.gl/3gNQP4` to access the code.

Now, we'll create a new Azure Function as a part of our serverless architecture that listens to HTTP requests to a certain address. It will listen to HTTP requests to a certain address as its trigger. Let's begin by implementing the following steps:

1. Create a new solution. The example is called `BeginningAzureServerlessArchitecture`, which is a logical wrapper for several functions that will get deployed to that namespace.

2. Use the **Visual C#** | **Cloud** | **Azure Function** template. Select the **Empty trigger** type and leave the default options, but set storage to **None**. This will create a Function App, which is a logical wrapper for several functions that will get deployed and scaled together:

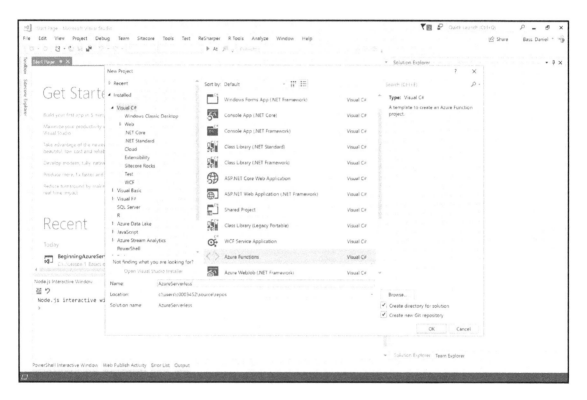

3. You now have a solution with two files in it: `host.json` and `local.settings.json`. The `local.settings.json` file is used solely for local development, where it stores all of the details on connections to other Azure services.

When uploading something to a public repository, be very careful not to commit unencrypted connection settings—by default, they will be unencrypted. `host.json` is the only file required to configure any functions running as part of your Function App. This file can have settings that control the function timeout, security settings for every function, and a lot more.

4. Now, right-click on the project and select **Add New Item**. Once again, choose the **Azure Function** template:

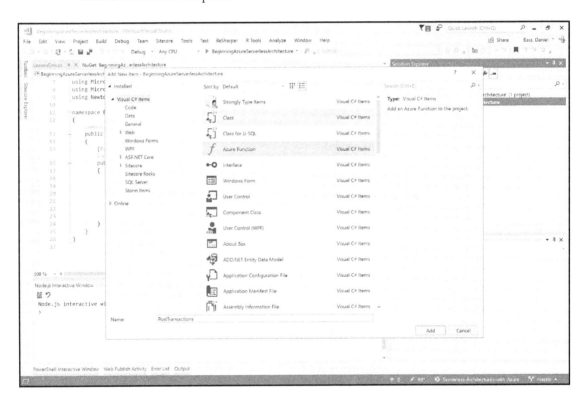

5. On the next screen, select **Http trigger with parameters** and **Access rights** should be set to **Anonymous**. Right-click on your solution and select **Enable NuGet Package Restore**:

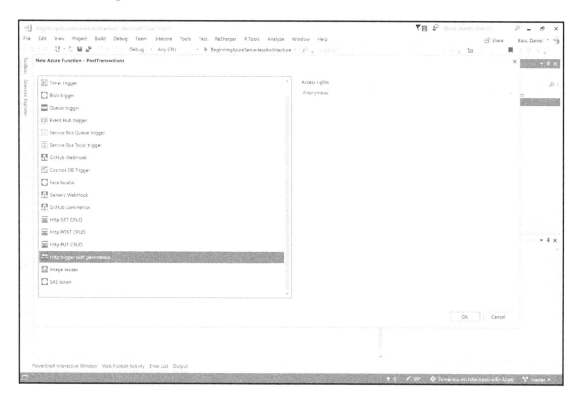

 An important thing to remember is that this template is different from the first one you used, because it is inside the solution. Call it `PostTransactions`, or something similar.

6. You will now have a C# file called `PostTransactions.cs`. It consists of a single method, `Run`, with an awful lot in the method signature: an attribute and an annotation. Some of this will be familiar to you if you are an experienced C# developer, and it is important to understand this signature.

Refer to the code for this example placed at `Code/Serverless-Architectures-with-Azure/Lesson 1/BeginningAzureServerlessArchitecture/PostTransactionsEx A.cs`. Go to `https://goo.gl/iCt7dG` to access the code.

Configuration as code is an important modern development practice. Rather than having servers reconfigured or configured manually by developers before code is deployed to them, configuration as code dictates that all of the configuration required to deploy an application to production be included in the source code.

This allows for variable replacement by your build/release agent, as you will (understandably) want slightly different settings, depending on your environment.

Azure Functions implement this principle, with a configuration split between the `host.json` file for app-wide configurations and app settings, and the `Run` method signature for individual functions. Therefore, you can deploy an Azure Function to production with only the code that you find in the GitHub repository:

```csharp
using System.Net;
using System.Net.Http;
using Microsoft.Azure.WebJobs;
using Microsoft.Azure.WebJobs.Extensions.Http;
using Microsoft.Azure.WebJobs.Host;

namespace BeginningAzureServerlessArchitecture
{
    public static class PostTransactions
    {
        [FunctionName("PostTransactions")]
        public static HttpResponseMessage Run([HttpTrigger(
            AuthorizationLevel.Anonymous,
            "get",
            "post",
            Route = "PostTransactions/name/{name}")] HttpRequestMessage req, string name, TraceWriter log)
        {
            log.Info("C# HTTP trigger function processed a request.");

            // Fetching the name from the path parameter in the request URL
            return req.CreateResponse(HttpStatusCode.OK, "Hello " + name);
        }
    }
}
```

Outcome

You created an Azure Function, understood the roles the different files play, and learned about configuration as code.

The `FunctionName` annotation defines the name of the function within the Function App.

This can be used for triggering your function, or it can be kept separate. The first parameter is an `HttpRequestMessage` object with an `HttpTrigger` attribute. This is what varies when you choose different triggers (for example, a timer trigger will have an object with a `TimerTrigger` attribute).

This attribute has several arguments. The first is the authorization level. Do you remember setting this when you created the function? It was called **Access rights** in the template. This defines the level of authorization that the function will demand of HTTP requests. The five levels are shown in the following table:

Authorization level	Required information
Anonymous	No key required; anyone with the path can call it an unlimited number of times.
User	Need a valid token, generated by a user that has AD permission to trigger the Function App. Useful for high-security environments, where each service needs to manage its own security. Generally, token-based authentication is much more desirable than key-based.
Function	Need the function key—a unique key created for each function in a Function App upon deployment. Any host key will also work. The most common form of authorization for basic deployments.
System	Need the master key—a key at the Function App level (called a **host key**) that cannot be deleted, but can be renewed.
Admin	Need any host key.

 One thing to bear in mind is that if you set a function to be high security and use **System** or **Admin** authorization, then any client that you give that key to will also be able to access any other functions in the Function App (if they can work out the path). Make sure that you separate high-security functions into different apps. An improved approach is discussed in the next chapter—using Azure Active Directory.

The next parameters are GET and POST, which define the HTTP verbs that will activate the function. Generally, from a microservices architecture point of view, you should only have one verb, to prevent you from having to do bug-prone switching logic inside of the function. You can simply create four separate functions if you want `GET`, `POST`, `PUT`, and `DELETE` on an artifact.

Finally, there is a string assigned to the property route. This is the only bit of routing logic that the function itself can see, and it simply defies the subpath from the Function App. It accepts WebAPI syntax, which you can see in the curly braces, / {name}. This will assign any text that appears where the curly braces are to a parameter called name.

This completes the HttpTrigger object. Other types of triggers, which we will touch on later, have different objects and different constructors. The three parameters left in the method signature are an HttpRequestMessage object, which allows you to access the HttpRequestMessage that triggered the function; a string parameter called name, which is what the string in the curly braces in the path will get bound to; and a TraceWriter for logging.

The current logic of the Function App can be seen in the following example, and you should see that it will take whatever name is put into it and send back an HTTP response saying Hello to that name. We will test this out in the next subtopic.

Debugging an Azure Function

You now have a working Azure Function that can be deployed to Azure or run locally. We will first host and debug the function locally, to show the development cycle in action. At the moment, its logic is very basic and not particularly useful, so we will be developing this to store some data in a cloud-hosted database over the rest of the chapter.

Debug an Azure Function

In this section, we'll run an Azure Function locally and debug it. We'll be developing new functions and test the functionality before deploying to public cloud. And to ensure that it happens correctly, we'll require the single function created directly from the HTTP trigger with **parameters** template.

Currently, your machine does not have the correct runtime to run an Azure Function, so we need to download it:

1. Click the **Play** button in Visual Studio, and a dialog box should ask you if you want to download **Azure Functions Core Tools**—click on **Yes**. A Windows CMD window will open, with the lightning bolt logo of Azure Functions:

 It will bootstrap the environment and attach the debugger from Visual Studio. It will then list the endpoints the Function App is listening on.

2. Open up Postman app and copy and paste the endpoint into it, selecting either a POST or GET verb.

 You should get the response `Hello {name}`. Try changing the `{name}` in the path to your name, and you will see a different response.
You can download Postman at `https://www.getpostman.com/`.

3. Create a debug point in the Run method by clicking in the margin to the left of the code:

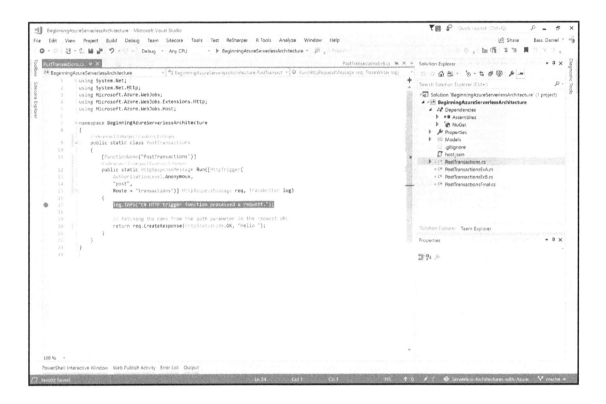

Refer to the code for this example placed at `Code/Serverless-Architectures-with-Azure/Lesson 1/BeginningAzureServerlessArchitecture/PostTransactionsEx A.cs`.

Go to `https://goo.gl/iCt7dG` to access the code.

4. Use Postman to send the request:

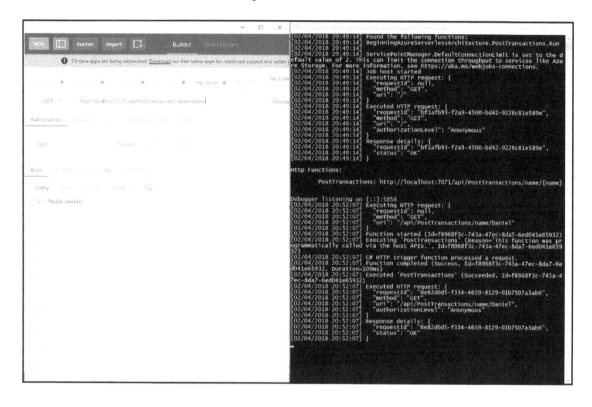

5. You are now able to use standard Visual Studio debugging features and inspect the different objects as shown in the following screenshot:

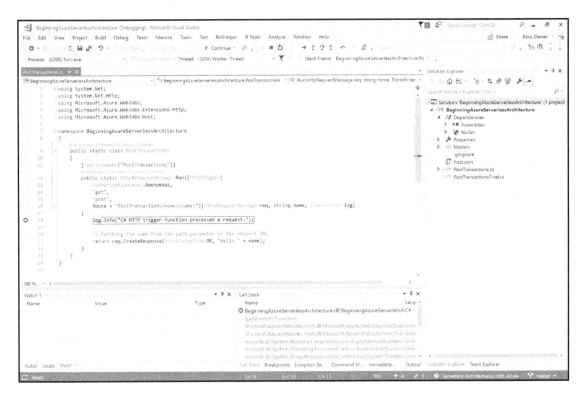

6. Set your verb to POST , and add a message in the payload. See if you can find the verb in the HttpRequestMessage object in debug mode. It should be in the method property.

If you need to download Azure-functions-core-tools separately, you can use npm command to download it—npm install -g azure-functions-core-tools for version 1 (fully supported) and npm install -g azure-functions-core-tools@core for version 2 (beta). We will go into the differences in versions later in this chapter. You can then use the debug setup to set Visual Studio to call an external program with the command func host start when you click on the **Debug** button.

Outcome

You have debugged an Azure Function and tested it using Postman.

As you can see from running the function locally, you, the developer, do not need to write any of the usual boilerplate code for message handling or routing. You don't even need to use ASP.NET controllers, or set up middleware. The Azure Functions container handles absolutely everything, leaving your code to simply do the business logic.

Activity: Improving Your Function

In this activity, we will add a JSON payload to the request and write code to parse that message into a C# object.

Prerequisites

You will require a function created from the HTTP trigger with the parameters template.

Scenario

You are creating the start of a personal finance application that allows users to add their own transactions, integrate with other applications and perhaps allow their credit card to directly log transactions. It will be able to scale elastically to any number of users, saving us money when we don't have any users.

Aim

Parse a JSON payload into a C# object, starting your RESTful API.

Steps for Completion

1. Change the **Route** to **transactions**.
2. Remove the `get` verb. Remove the String parameter called `name`:

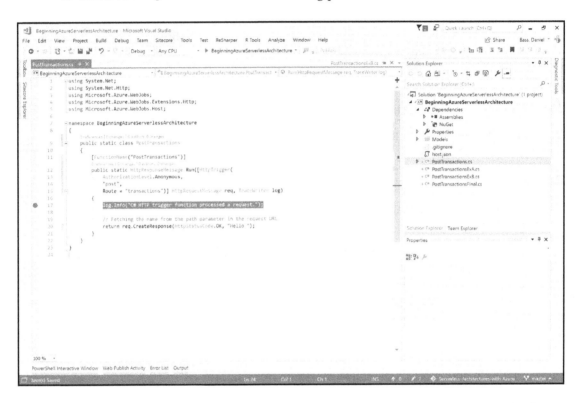

3. Add the `Newtonsoft.json` package, if it isn't already present. You can do this by right-clicking the **Solution | Manage NuGet packages | Browse | Newtonsoft.Json**.

 Version 10.0.3 is used for this book.

4. Right-click on the project and add a folder called `Models`, then add a C# class called `Transaction`. Add two properties to this class: a `DateTime` property called `ExecutionTime`, and a `Decimal` property called `Amount`:

Refer to the complete code placed at `Code/Serverless-Architectures-with-Azure/Lesson 1/BeginningAzureServerlessArchitecture/Models/Transaction.cs`.

Go to `https://goo.gl/H6cu2M` to access the code.

5. Use `JsonConvert.DeserializeObject<Transaction>(message).Result(` `)` to deserialize the `HttpRequestMessage` into an instantiation of this class. To do that, you need to import the `Models` namespace and `Newtonsoft.Json`. This will parse the JSON payload and use the `Amount` property to file the corresponding property on the `Transaction` object:

Refer to the complete code placed at `Code/Serverless-Architectures-with-Azure/Lesson 1/BeginningAzureServerlessArchitecture/PostTransactionsExC.cs`.

Go to `https://goo.gl/ttyvpT` to access the code.

6. Change the return message to use a property of the new `Transaction` object, for example, `You entered a transaction of £47.32!` Go to Postman and open the **Body** tab and select **raw**.

7. Enter in the following JSON object:

```
{
  Amount: 47.32,
  ExecutionTime: "2018-01-01T09:00:00Z"
}
```

8. Run locally to test. Make sure you change the endpoint to /transactions in Postman.

Outcome

You have learned how to access the HttpRequestMessage, and you will have a function that can read a JSON message and turn it into a C# object.

During this subtopic, you debugged an Azure Function. Visual Studio only allows this through downloading azure-functions-core-tools. Unfortunately, it doesn't make it available on the general command line—only through command windows started in Visual Studio. If you want to use it independently, then you have to download it using npm. If you need to download azure-functions-core-tools separately, you can use npm to get it—npm install -g azure-functions-core-tools for version 1 (fully supported) and npm install -g azure-functions-core-tools@core for version 2 (beta). We will go into the differences in versions later in this chapter. You can then use the debug setup to set Visual Studio to call an external program with the command func host start when you click on the **Debug** button.

This package is a lot more than just a debug environment, however; it actually has a CLI for everything you could possibly need in Azure Function development. Open up a command window (in Visual Studio, if you haven't downloaded it independently) and type func help; you should see a full list of everything the CLI can do. Notable commands are func host start, which starts the local debug environment, and func azure {functionappname} fetch-app-settings, which lets you download the app settings of a function deployed to Azure so that you can test integration locally, as well. These need to be run in the same folder as the host.json file.

 Developing in Visual Studio is much easier for Azure Functions, especially if it is your usual IDE, but it's perfectly possible to use a simple text editor and the CLI to develop. If you are developing for version 2 on a Mac or Linux machine, this setup is basically the only way to develop at the moment, although Visual Studio Code has a good Azure Functions extension.

Deploying an Azure Function

An Azure Function is obviously geared towards being hosted on the Azure cloud, rather than locally or on your own computer. Visual Studio comes with a complete suite of tools to deploy and manage Azure services, and this includes full support for Azure Functions. The `azure-functions-core-tools` CLI that you downloaded to provide a local debug environment also has a set of tools for interacting with Azure Functions in the cloud, if you prefer CLIs. We will focus on using Visual Studio, but we will mention some of the equivalent methods in the CLI.

It is possible to run Azure Functions on your own servers, using the Azure Functions runtime. This is a good way to utilize the sunk cost that you have already spent on servers, combined with the unlimited scale that Azure offers (if demand exceeds your server capacity). It's probably only worth it in terms of cost if you have a significant amount of unused Windows server time, because this solution inevitably requires more management than normal Azure Function deployments.

To deploy to Azure, you will need an Azure login with a valid Azure subscription.

Deploying to Azure

In this section, we'll deploy our first function to the public cloud, and learn how to call it. We'll be going live with our Azure Function, starting to create our serverless architecture. And to ensure that it happens correctly, we'll need a function project and a valid Azure subscription. Let's begin by implementing the following steps:

1. Right-click on your project and select **Publish....** Now select **Azure Function App** | **Create New** as shown in the following screenshot:

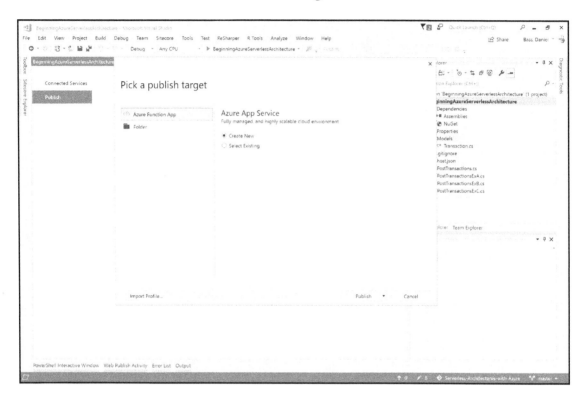

 If you've signed in to Visual Studio with a Microsoft ID that has an Azure subscription associated with it, then the next screen will be pre-populated with a subscription. If not, then you need to sign in to an account with an associated Azure subscription.

2. Enter a memorable name and create a resource group and a consumption app service plan to match the following:

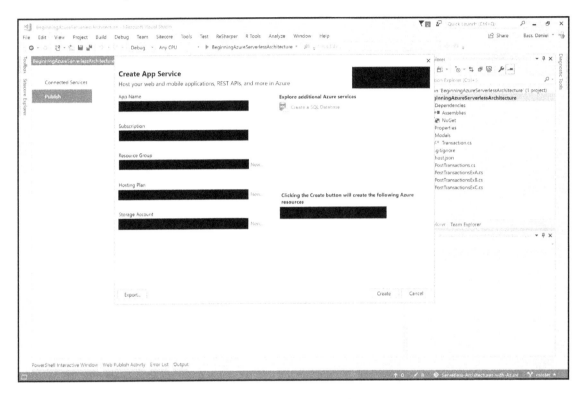

3. Click on the **Publish** button to publish your function.
4. Open a browser, navigate to `http://portal.azure.com`, and find your function. You can use the search bar and search the name of your function. Click on your Function App, then click on the function name. Click the **Get function URL** in the upper-right corner paste the address of your function into Postman, and test it. Please bear in mind that if you have a paid subscription, these executions will cost a small amount of money—you are only charged for the compute resources that you actually use. On a free account, you get a million executions for free.

Outcome

You now have a fully deployed and working Azure Function in the cloud.

This is not the recommended way to deploy to production. **Azure Resource Manager** (**ARM**) templates are the recommended way to deploy to production. ARM templates are **JavaScript Object Notation** (**JSON**) files. The resources that you want to deploy are declaratively described within JSON. An ARM template is idempotent, which means it can be run as many times as required, and the output will be the same each and every time. Azure handles the execution and targets the changes that need to be run.

Anyone can execute your function if they can work out the address, which is why the security we discussed previously is a good idea to implement. We will further discuss the optimal way to employ security for a large enterprise using Azure Active Directory in the next chapter.

The old way of deploying Azure Functions allowed you to edit the C# code in the portal, but all of those sections will come up as read-only. For proper development, you should rarely even interact with the portal; everything is possible in Visual Studio with the Cloud Explorer.

You can remote debug Azure Functions using the **Cloud Explorer**. Click **View Menu** | **Cloud Explorer** and log in to your Azure account. Find your function under **App Services**. Select the function in the **Cloud Explorer**, and click **Attach Debugger**.

Technical Basis of Azure Functions

So, we successfully created an Azure Function, ran it on a local environment, and deployed it to the cloud.

Azure Functions run on servers that have Azure WebJobs installed on them. Azure WebJobs allow DLLs, or any supported code, to be hot-swapped in and take advantage of deep Azure integrations.

We'll cover the two runtimes in more depth now, but the key takeaway is that there is a fully-supported, Windows-based version, and also a beta cross-platform version. Microsoft are pushing towards the cross-platform version.

Version 1 is based on Azure WebJobs, which is written in C# and .NET. Azure WebJobs is essentially a service with a set of adapters for Azure products. These adapters usually go a lot deeper than a standard API. When code is deployed into it, Azure WebJobs reads `host.json` to create an environment with the same context every time. When you downloaded `azure-functions-core-tools`, it contained a full production Azure Functions environment, exactly the same as the ones used in Azure. That is why we can only develop on Windows machines for version 1.

Version 2 is based on the new Azure WebJobs, written in C# and .NET Core. It can run on any server that supports .NET Core, which includes all major distributions of Linux, as well as Windows.

.NET Core is significantly faster than .NET and can run on any platform, allowing Microsoft to allocate more types of servers to Azure Functions work.

Rewriting Azure WebJobs in .NET Core will remove support for the plethora of semi-supported, experimental languages, like Python and PowerShell, but will add Java support.

Executing and Scaling Azure Functions

The containers that Azure Functions run in are inherently short-lived, with a maximum execution time of 10 minutes allowed (this was set in `host.json`, as seen earlier), but it is generally advisable to execute HTTP requests in two minutes. This short timeframe is part of what allows for the flexibility of Azure Functions, so if you need longer execution times but still want most of the convenience of serverless computing, then look at using Azure WebJobs SDK, running on a VM or physical machine that you control, or Azure Data Lake Analytics, if you are processing large datasets.

The resources that Azure allocates to functions is set at the Function App level, split equally among functions inside that app. Most of the time, this will have absolutely no practical impact on your work, and generally, you should keep logically connected functions in the same app. However, in cases where you suddenly demand massive scaling for one of your functions but not for the others, this can cause issues. If your suddenly popular function is one of twenty in an app, it's going to take longer to allocate enough resources to supply it. On the other hand, if you have a seldom-used function that you need better latency from, consider adding it to the Function App of a commonly-used one, so that the function doesn't have to warm up from the cold.

Activity: Creating a Function That Stores User Detail

Prerequisites

You will need Visual Studio installed, with Azure development workload.

Scenario

Creating a personalized application for users.

Aim

Create a function that stores user details.

Steps for Completion

1. Create a new function, called `PostUser`, using the `HttpTrigger` template. If you are competent in another language, like JavaScript or F#, you can try creating it in that language.
2. Create a new model called `User`. Think about what properties you'd like to include, but as a minimum, you will need an email address and a unique identifier (these can be the same property).
3. Modify the function to decode a JSON-formatted request into this model.

Outcome

You have a function ready to store user details.

Refer to the complete code placed at `Code/Serverless-Architectureswith-Azure/Lesson 3/BeginningAzureServerlessArchitecture/Models/`.

Before the transactions have taken place: `User.cs`: https://goo.gl/9FpHce.

After the transactions have taken place: `PostUsers.cs`: https://goo.gl/CWxA2S.

Summary

In this chapter, you covered the benefits and disadvantages of serverless computing. Next, you learned how to create, debug, and deploy an Azure Function, Azure's primary serverless product. This is the basic building block of serverless applications, and the first step to creating fully serverless architectures. Finally, you learned about the technical basis of Azure Functions, and how you can utilize your knowledge of it to improve the performance of your functions.

In the next chapter, we will be covering integrations with other Azure services and Azure-based logging and security solutions.

Deploying Azure Serverless

2

Most of what was covered in the previous chapter could apply to any serverless product; even runtimes that seem unique are fairly similar. You can easily find analogues for most of the previous chapter in AWS or Google Cloud. In this chapter, you will learn about Azure-specific features. You'll integrate your function with other Azure services to create a serverless RESTful API. Azure Application Insights will also be integrated into your solution, providing your support team with unparalleled data about what your application is doing. Finally, your serverless functions will be secured using API keys, to prevent unauthorized use.

By the end of this chapter, you will be able to:

- Integrate an Azure Function with Cosmos DB
- Combine a complete logging and monitoring solution with Azure Application Insights
- Secure your Azure Functions using API keys
- Integrate with an Azure App Service

Integrating with Other Azure Services

As a developer, you are constantly asked if your service can talk to a new product. There is an emphasis on moving from the walled garden architecture of old to open, modular, easy-to-integrate services. Even software companies are struggling to catch up with this new demand, with many products still shipping as closed systems, without basic API layers.

So far, Cosmos DB has been mentioned several times in this book, but what is it? It's Microsoft's flagship cloud database. It's a fully elastic, dynamically resourced database which is schema agnostic. It has multiple APIs available. It has a native SQL API, which supports JSON documents, a MongoDB API, a Cassanda API, a Graph API and a Key-Value pair API. It can be tuned to maximum performance/parallelism and lower consistency, or back to the more traditional **Atomicity, Consistency, Isolation, Durability (ACID)** compliant model, with five separate models. It is certainly great for building applications quickly, and knowing that you will never, ever have a scaling issue.

A NoSQL database, like Cosmos DB, does not behave like a SQL database, but it does have similar concepts. Cosmos DB has a database, which is a group of collections. Collections are the approximate equivalent of tables in SQL databases. Inside collections there are documents which are the approximate equivalent of records in SQL databases. NoSQL databases have distinct advantages in performance at high scale and geographic spread because they can be horizontally scaled. Each server instance holds a copy of all of the documents in the database (or a subset thereof), and communicates with the other servers when one of its documents is edited. If you stick to ACID compliance, all other servers will be blocked from making edits when a single edit comes in. If you relax the consistency, it removes some of the blocks, allowing greater performance at the cost of consistency.

There is a very straightforward way to integrate Azure Functions with Cosmos DB, using the standard C# library.

Inserting Documents into Cosmos DB

This section will discuss inserting documents into a Cosmos DB. It will leverage the near-infinite scale of Cosmos DB to deliver a planet-scale serverless application. And to ensure that it happens correctly, you will need a function in the state from the previous chapter and an Azure subscription with the ability to set up a Cosmos DB. Let's begin by implementing the following steps:

1. Right-click on your project and select **Manage NuGet Packages....** Install version 1.0.0 of `MicrosoftAzure.WebJobs.Extensions.DocumentDB`.

   DocumentDB is the old name for Cosmos DB; Microsoft haven't updated all of the SDKs yet. There's an SDK with the new name, but it's still in beta.

   Refer to the complete code at: `Code/ServerlessArchitectures-with-Azure/Lesson 2/BeginningAzureServerlessArchitecture/PostTransactionsEx AStart.cs`

   Go to `https://goo.gl/KEFP7K` to access the code.

2. Add a line to the method signature, as shown in the following screenshot:

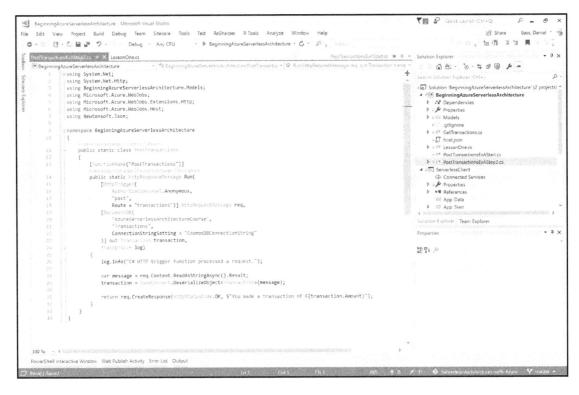

The attribute DocumentDB dictates that the output of this function will be a document written into Cosmos DB. The first argument is the database to use, and the second argument is the collection. The third argument is a piece of good practice.

By default, the Azure Function will use an app setting called `AzureWebJobsDocumentDBConnectionString` to connect to the Cosmos DB. Given that it's no longer called DocumentDB, it's going to be pretty confusing to keep it as that, so this variable tells the function to look in the app settings for a variable with a different name.

3. Create a Cosmos DB instance in the Azure portal. Choose the SQL API. It might take a little while to create.

4. Create a database called `AzureServerlessArchitectureCourse` and a collection called `Transactions`. Set the size to 10 GB fixed, and set the RU/s to the lowest amount possible:

The 10 GB fixed setting is good for development instances to make sure you're aren't accidentally overfilling the database due to a bug in your code. RU/s are **Request Units**, so the more you have of these, the more concurrent requests your database can serve. Cosmos DB is charged on storage and request units separately.

5. Add an entry to `local.settings.json` with the name `CosmosDBConnectionString`, and copy and paste the connection string from the **Keys** section of your Cosmos DB instance in the portal:

6. Finally, set the dynamic object to be the instance of the object deserialized from JSON. Make sure the `Transaction` class is public.
7. Run it locally in order to test it. Submit at least 3 valid transactions—this is important for the next example.
8. Click on the **Publish** button to publish your function to Azure.
9. Go to your Function App in the portal, click on **Application settings** and enter a new application setting, matching your settings in your `local.settings.json`.
10. Test the function that's been deployed to Azure.

Outcome

To have linked an Azure Function to Cosmos DB, successfully inserting documents.

Retrieving Data from Cosmos DB

In this section, we'll retrieve documents from the Cosmos DB for display or manipulation. We have deployed Cosmos DB with transactions in the collection:

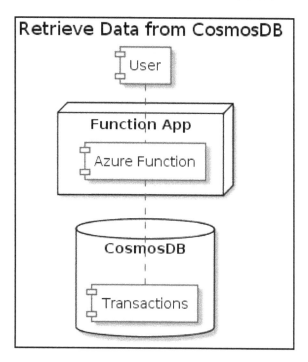

Let's begin by implementing the following steps:

1. Create an Azure Function called `GetTransactions` and use the `HttpTrigger` template without parameters and `Anonymous` access rights.

2. Add the line shown in the following screenshot to the method signature. You are adding a `DocumentDB` client as an input to the function, below the trigger. This allows you to execute more complex queries against DocumentDB:

3. Next, you need to set some options for your query, setting the max amount of records the Cosmos DB will return. Remove the code inside the `Run` method. Create a `FeedOptions` object and set `MaxItemCount` to –1 (allowing dynamic page size):

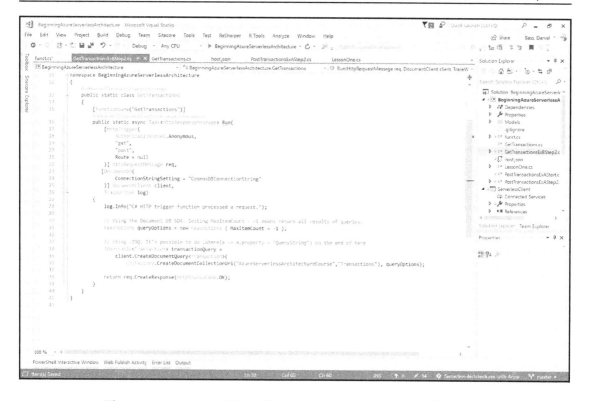

The `FeedOptions` object allows you to set options for things like which partition to search in and the maximum degree of parallelism for Cosmos DB to operate at.

Refer to the complete code placed at: `Code/Serverless-Architectures-with-Azure/Lesson 2/BeginningAzureServerlessArchitecture/GetTransactionsExB Step2.cs`.

Go to `https://goo.gl/e3dAqx` to access the code.

4. Create the query. Use the `CreateDocumentQuery` method on the `DocumentClient` object. There is a helper method for creating the collection `uri` that it demands in `UriFactory.CreateDocumentCollectionUri`. Finally, pass in the `FeedOptions` object that you created before:

Refer to the complete code placed at: `Code/Serverless-Architectures-with-Azure/Lesson 2/BeginningAzureServerlessArchitecture/GetTransactionsExB Step5.cs`.

Go to `https://goo.gl/aZybgD` to access the code.

5. Execute the query against Cosmos DB by creating a `foreach` loop through each transaction in the `IQueryable` result. Add each to a list of transactions:

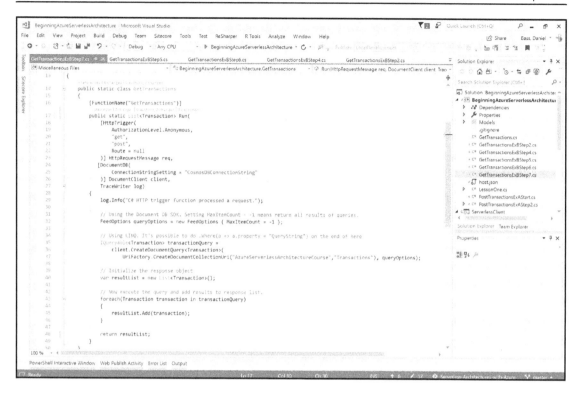

Refer to the complete code placed at: `Code/Serverless-Architectures-with-Azure/Lesson 2/BeginningAzureServerlessArchitecture/GetTransactionsExBStep7.cs`.

Go to `https://goo.gl/A7pyzk` to access the code.

If you test this function with Postman, you will see the transactions that you previously entered into the Cosmos DB. You now have a completely serverless RESTful API. This requires no operational setup up of containers or **virtual machines** (**VMs**). The API will scale infinitely, along with the database behind it, for any use case. A schema has effectively been enforced by the use of C# objects on the API, so you can rely upon whatever you receive from it, despite it being stored in a NoSQL database.

It's still a good idea to add more complete error handling to avoid unexpected objects from the Cosmos DB causing problems.

A RESTful web service is one that implements the **Representational State Transfer (REST)** architectural style. This is a very popular architectural style on the web.

Outcome

You have linked an Azure Function to Cosmos DB and successfully retrieved the documents.

One of the interesting developments of the Microservices architecture movement is the concept of monetizing APIs. The idea is that your information is valuable, and as such you can charge for access to your APIs. Most organizations settle for charging for API keys, with few having the data granularity to charge by request. But how do you set that price? Serverless offers a great indicator, because you can literally see how much each request is costing you. There is no sunk cost offsetting that price either, so pricing your APIs at a certain profit margin above that cost is enough to make the service profitable.

Read up on microservices architecture at: `https://docs.microsoft.com/en-us/azure/architecture/guide/architecture-styles/microservices`.

Logging with Application Insights

One of the most important operational requirements for software is that your company understand what the application is doing and can triage responses to errors. This is generally achieved via some form of logging, and there is a service in Azure for this, called **Application Insights**. It's a very sophisticated application health monitoring tool that combines out-of-the-box monitoring, like processor loads, RAM usage, and errors, with specific logging that the developer has to implement. While Azure Functions don't really have concerns with processor loads or RAM usage, it useful to know the average length of calls, how many instances are being spun up, and hourly spend.

In the next example, you will add Azure Application Insights integration to your previous two functions, to enable effective support.

Integrating Azure Application Insights

In this section, we'll add logging to your Azure Functions using Azure Application Insights. We'll need to receive vital information about what our software is doing, so that we can triage issues. And to ensure that it happens correctly, we'll need the Azure Functions created earlier. Let's begin by implementing the following steps:

1. Create an **Application Insights** instance by going on to the portal and creating one from the marketplace. Use the .NET app setting. Note down the instrumentation key from the overview panel; you'll need it later.

2. Install a NuGet package, `Microsoft.ApplicationInsights`.

3. Add the line of code in the screenshot (the private static string with the application insights key in it) to `PostTransactions.cs`. Then, create a private static `TelemetryClient`, using that key for its `InstrumentationKey` property.

Refer to the complete code placed at: `Code/Serverless-Architectures-with-Azure/Lesson 2/BeginningAzureServerlessArchitecture/PostTransactionsExCStep3.cs`.

Go to `https://goo.gl/AFwL27` to access the code.

For local development, it can be easier to just copy and paste your instrumentation key directly into the `TelemetryClient`. In production, you should use app settings, which would be controlled by a variable in your release process:

4. Import `MicrosoftExtensions.Logging`. Change the `TraceWriter` to an `ILogger`.

5. Change all of the previous log methods to `LogInformation`:

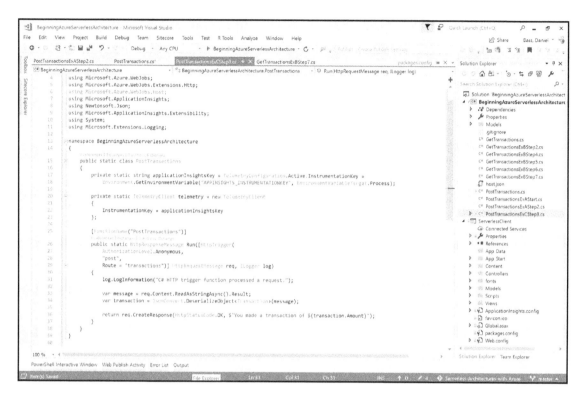

6. Wrap your `JsonConvert.DeserializeObject` statement in a `try-catch` block. In the `catch` block, log that there has been an error with log `LogError()`. Next, track the event of a bad request with `telemetry.TrackEvent()` and track the exception using `telemetry.TrackException(e)`. Finally, return a `BadRequest` HTTP response.

7. Add a null check on the object inside the `try` block—this is in case `Newtonsoft.Json` fails quietly. Throw an exception if the object is null. You could also check individual properties and throw exceptions for them:

8. Deploy to Azure, go to the app settings of the Function App, and add the setting `APPINSIGHTS_INSTRUMENTATIONKEY;` with the key you got earlier.

> The Application Insights Key identifies your individual instance of Application Insights. This essentially just identifies your account to the underlying shared Application Insights architecture and ensures you only see your apps logs and no-one else's.
>
> Link for the code: `https://raw.githubusercontent.com/ TrainingByPackt/Serverless-Architectures-with-Azure/master/ Lesson%202O2/BeginningAzureServerlessArchitecture/ PostTransactionsExCStep6.cs.`

Outcome

Azure Functions submitted logs to Azure Application Insights. Now that you are successfully submitting logs to Application Insights, it's time to see what insights we can get from this and how we might action them. Hopefully, you can see that when incorrectly formatted JSON payloads are submitted to the function, we will be tracking that exception, so we will have a look at how to observe those logs. If you can imagine the situation of having an **Application Insights** dashboard on a screen in your office and seeing a series of malformed payload exceptions appear, the following steps would allow you to study the cause of that error and troubleshoot it.

Troubleshooting the Azure Function using Application Insights

In this section, we'll understand the process of identifying errors using Application Insights by implementing the following steps:

1. Add your Application Insights key to the **values** section of your local `settings.json` with the name `APPINSIGHTS_INSTRUMENTATIONKEY`. Create a request in Postman with any text in it (that won't deserialize successfully) and submit it to the local `PostTransactions` function address.

2. Open `https://portal.azure.com` and navigate to the Azure Application Insights instance.

3. In the overview screen, there are a series of charts and buttons. The most useful ones are the average response time graphs and the **Alerts** widget—these give you a quick way of assessing if there's an issue with your function.

4. Select the button on the top ribbon that says **Analytics**.

5. You are now in the metrics query editor. Choose the pre-canned **errors** query in the bottom right and execute it. You can see the error from your malformed payload. You could then use the information provided to troubleshoot the problem.

6. Return to the **Overview** page and select **Metric Explorer**.

7. Select an empty graph and click the absolutely tiny edit button in the top right.

8. Expand the errors arrow and check the exceptions box. The graph should now show a spike corresponding to the error you just caused with Postman.

The metrics explorer section you used in the final stage of this example allowed you to set up quick, easy to read graphs that will display any change in normal operations. It's likely you'd want to categorize a bad payload as a custom exception so as to separate it from more genuine exceptions with your code—this is where you'd filter them out.

The metrics section is more fine-grained, with a SQL-like syntax allowing you to select individual error records. Once you've been alerted to a problem, this is where you would go to find the exception message and start your troubleshooting.

Security with API Keys

The standard way of securing APIs on the Internet is through the use of keys and secrets, and a serverless API is no different. You should secure every function you create with at least function-level authorization, unless there is a compelling argument for it being public. You should definitely secure your data-input APIs and any output APIs with sensitive information on them. Public-facing APIs are an interesting case for serverless, because you are charged per request. This means that a malicious actor could DDoS your public function and hit you where it hurts the wallet. Friendly users with valid keys could inadvertently do this as well if they don't rate-limit their requests. A good solution to this, and a generally good solution for API's in general, is to use an API proxy. Microsoft has one called the **Azure API Gateway**, or there are other services like Apigee or MuleSoft.

 It's important to understand the reason to secure a serverless function. Other than the usual reasons for preventing normal malicious access, the serverless pricing model presents an interesting target for hackers: they can repeatedly call your serverless function and deplete your bank account when your cloud provider charges according to resources used.

Creating a Client with Azure Application Service

In this section, we'll use an Azure Application Service to call an unsecured Azure Function. We'll be creating a new client application to use your serverless backend. This will allow our users to see the money management application on the internet. And to ensure that it happens correctly, we'll need to deploy Azure Serverless RESTful API. Let's begin by implementing the following steps:

1. Create a new project using the ASP.NET Web application template called **ServerlessClient**. Choose **MVC** with **No Authentication**.

2. Create a new MVC 5 controller with read/write actions, called `TransactionController`, and a new model called `Transaction` (you can copy the earlier one, but make sure to change the namespace).

You can find the for Transaction model here: `https://github.com/TrainingByPackt/Serverless-Architectures-with-Azure/blob/master/Lesson%202/BeginningAzureServerlessArchitecture/Models/Transaction.cs`

3. Then, right-click on the top Index function in the controller and select **Add | View...**.
4. Call the view `Index`, set the **Template** to **List** and set the view model to **Transaction**. Finally, set the **View** to **Partial**.
5. Delete all of the HTML in the **Home/Index** view, and replace it with the code in the following screenshot to reference the partial view:

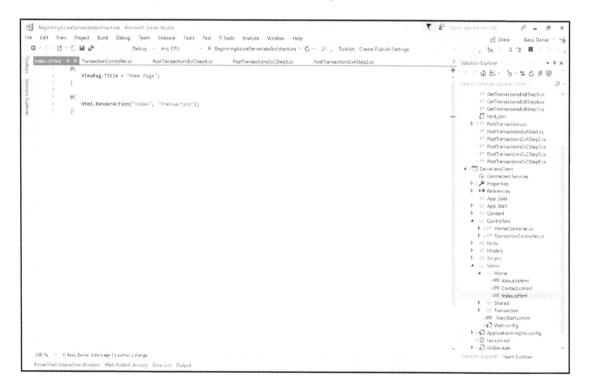

Refer to the complete code placed at:
`Code/ServerlessArchitectures-with-Azure/Lesson 2/ServerlessClient/Views/Home/Index.cshtml`.

Go to `https://goo.gl/u2snyb` to access the code.

6. Call the address of the serverless `GET` function in the `Index` method and map the JSON object into the Model and View, as in the preceding screenshot. There's some helpful code for debugging the front end that has been commented out:

Refer to the complete code placed at:
`Code/ServerlessArchitectures-with-Azure/Lesson2/ServerlessClient/Controllers/TransactionControllerExDStep6.cs`

Go to `https://goo.gl/4kBpcW` to access the code.

7. Edit the view to display the information from the `transactions` model, and add the view to the index; test this now:

The Azure Application Service is calling unauthorized APIs.

You can now see the transactions that you previously entered into the database on your web app. You can also create transactions using Postman, and refresh the page and see them in your web app. Our web app is listing transactions, so this state of insecurity is clearly not acceptable. We'll add key-based security for the POST API, and you can see how to add it to the `GET` method in your own time.

Securing an Azure Function with an API key

In this section, we'll use an Azure Application Service to call an Azure Function secured with an API key. We want to protect a serverless function from malicious requests. And to ensure that it happens correctly, we'll need to deploy Azure Serverless RESTful API. Let's begin by implementing the following steps:

 If you haven't created an application setting for the Cosmos DB connection string you'll find it difficult to debug 500 errors. Also if you have different routes for `PostTransactions` and `GetTransactions` you'll need to make the function URL's different in the MVC controller.

1. Go to your function that creates new records in the Cosmos DB, and change the authorization level to **Function**. Deploy it to Azure.
2. Go to the portal and copy the key for the app. Test this in Postman by adding `?code=YourFunctionKey` on the end of the URL of the function.
3. Go to your `TransactionController` and select the **Create** method that should have been templated for you. Click **Add | View...**, and choose a **Partial View** called **Create** (with the **Create** template), using the `Transaction` model:

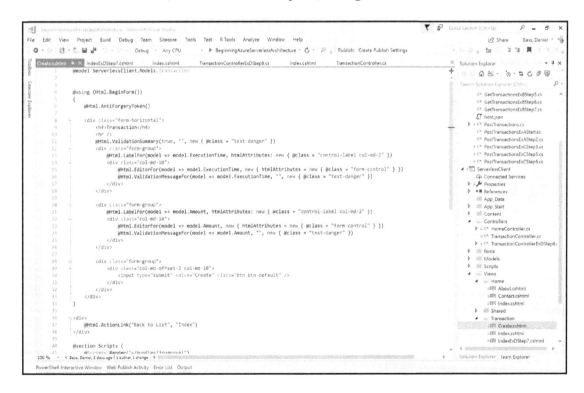

Refer to the complete code placed at:
`Code/ServerlessArchitectures-with-Azure/Lesson`
`2/ServerlessClient/Views/Transaction/Create.cshtml.`

Go to `https://goo.gl/if8F74` to access the code.

4. Add a reference to the view in the **Transaction Index** view after the list.
5. Change the `Create` POST function of the `TransactionController` to take a transaction object, convert it to JSON, and post it to the serverless function:

Refer to the complete code placed at:
`Code/ServerlessArchitectures-with-Azure/Lesson`
`2/ServerlessClient/Controllers/TransactionControllerExESt`
`ep5.cs.`

Go to `https://goo.gl/sL4Dbf` to access the code.

6. Add a `query` parameter to the URL of the function called `code`, with a value of your key for the function:

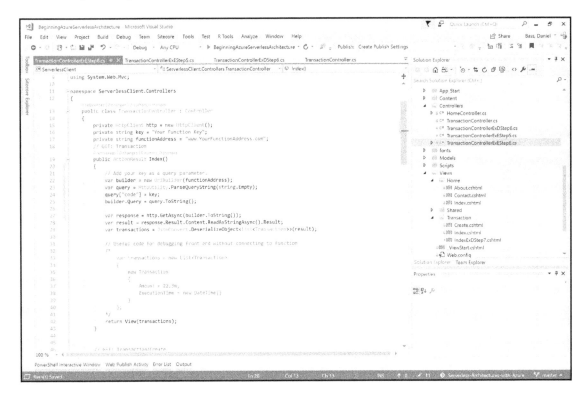

Refer to the complete code placed at:
`Code/ServerlessArchitectures-with-Azure/Lesson 2/ServerlessClient/Controllers/TransactionControllerExESt ep6.cs`

Go to `https://goo.gl/X3Z4cj` to access the code.

7. Test your form.
8. Deploy your web app to Azure using the **Publish** button. Set up a publish profile, creating a new app service in the same resource group as your function. (This is an optional step.)

Outcome

The secured serverless function is deployed in the cloud, being posted to by your web application.

Your API is now secured from any other applications or users accessing it directly. This is a very important level of protection for any API that allows the storing of data, because you don't want just anyone putting things into your database. You have also created a client application, which, while not quite qualifying as serverless, is deployed as a minimal management application with a runtime totally managed by Microsoft.

 It's also possible to secure your serverless code using Azure Active Directory. This can be a little complex to implement, as it's OAuth2-based, and therefore, likely to take too long for this book. More information can be found at: `https://docs.microsoft.com/en-us/azure/app-service/app-service-managed-service-identity?toc=%2fazure%2fazure-functions%2ftoc.json`.

Activity: Creating a Serverless Backend and Frontend for User Management

Prerequisites

The function from the previous activity.

Aim

Create a serverless backend and frontend for user management.

Scenario

Allowing your application to be used by multiple users, rather than just you.

Steps for Completion

1. Create a collection in the Cosmos DB to store your users. Alter your function so that it writes users to this collection.
2. Add a function to retrieve all of your users.
3. Add a screen to see all of the users of your application, and to create new users.

Outcome

Screen to store and manage users of the application.

 Refer to the complete code placed at `Code/Serverless-Architectureswith-Azure/Lesson3/BeginningAzureServerlessArchitecture/Models/`.

Before the transactions have taken place:

`User.cs`: `https://goo.gl/1C9PNt` to access the code.

`GetUsers.cs`: `https://goo.gl/oRH2WM` to access the code.

After the transactions have taken place:

`PostUsers.cs`: `https://goo.gl/JTh2Fc` to access the code.

Summary

In this chapter, you learned how to deploy a serverless API backed by an infinitely scalable database and fronted by an infinitely scalable web application. You covered more of the nuts and bolts of connecting serverless code to other services, along with logging and security considerations. Having the serverless code implement the API may feel like an over-complication at the moment (why not call the Cosmos DB directly from the controller of the MVC client application?), but the benefits of it being loosely coupled to the web application while the functions are also loosely coupled to each other will become apparent later.

Now that you've covered the basics of creating a simple architecture, we can add some more interesting features and components in the next chapter.

3
Architecting Serverless Solutions

Now that we have built an application backed by a serverless backend, we have a very basic serverless architecture.

These components can be triggered by a much greater variety of events than the HTTP requests that we used previously, from records being inserted into a SQL database, to the temperature dropping below a certain level. They allow you to wire together a massive variety of systems, executing simple code on the messages along the way, if required. Serverless can change the way you integrate systems together.

Azure Functions have a sister service, also serverless, that was made specifically for integrations between systems. The service is called **Azure Logic Apps**, and it has a fantastic selection of prebuilt adapters for all sorts of services, including non-Microsoft ones. You can create an Azure Logic App without opening Visual Studio or writing a single line of code; the apps have a simple drag-and-drop interface. This obviously leads to limitations for any kind of serious processing, so Logic Apps can trigger Azure Functions to do that processing for them. Azure Logic Apps and Azure Functions can be the glue that hold together an Azure Serverless architecture.

 Azure Logic Apps provide a means for application integration and workflow creation on cloud servers. It provides a graphical user interface for modifying the workflows. You can create a workflow with connectors and logic creation using inbuilt tools.

By the end of this chapter, you will be able to:

- Trigger actions based on inserted Cosmos DB documents
- Develop a weather-dependent notification for your personal finance app

- Analyze how to integrate old applications using serverless code
- Change the functionality from an old .NET app to an Azure Function

Architecting Greenfield Serverless Applications

A greenfield project (or product) is a new solution to a problem; it is not built on top of any existing application but usually is part of a wider business architecture.

Whenever a new greenfield project starts, technologists receive an often incomplete set of very approximate, high-level requirements. They then start to form an architecture to satisfy those requirements, and keep in mind any other requirements that they suspect may appear. Modern development approaches recognize the need for architecture to be as extensible and flexible as possible, because that initial set of requirements is never, ever complete, and today's greenfield projects are tomorrow's legacy systems.

 Techniques such as adding an API layer and making the subcomponents modular can be used to make applications flexible and extensible.

How can we extend this application? Well, we can add a function triggered by records added to the Cosmos DB.

Triggering Functions with Cosmos DB Records

In this section, we'll add a Cosmos DB triggered function, which is an independent and event-driven process, to our application. And to ensure that it happens correctly, there should be a Cosmos DB instance running. Let's begin by implementing the following steps:

1. Open Visual Studio and add a new function called `CosmosDBTriggered` to your Function App. Use the template **Cosmos DB Trigger**, and enter the same connection, database, and collection that we've been using for the `transactions` collection. Refer to the following screenshot:

 Refer to the complete code placed at `Code/Serverless-Architectures-with-Azure/Lesson 3/BeginningAzureServerlessArchitecture/CosmosDBTriggeredFunction.cs`.
Navigate to `https://goo.gl/Qc3sp8` to access the code.

Visual Studio will template a function out for you. This should be starting to look familiar. We have a **Cosmos DB Trigger** instead of an HTTP trigger this time. This will listen for records being updated or added to the collection. It does this by using a separate collection to keep track of leases. Basically, this is a collection that keeps track of events. The particulars of this technology are not something that we are going to go into today. The only aspect of it that you need to remember (for serverless) is that you need a different lease collection for each serverless function listening to events on the same collection.

2. Add a line saying `CreateLeaseCollectionIfNotExists = True`. This tells the function to create the collection, if it has not been created already:

Visual Studio may underline the **Cosmos DB Trigger** as not being recognized; if it does this go into **Manage NuGet Packages** and update all of the packages, except `Newtonsoft`.

3. Add an `HttpClient` inside the `If` statement, and create a `foreach` loop for each document in the input.

A query on Cosmos DB could insert or manipulate several records in one transaction.

4. Post a message asynchronously with a JSON copy of the document to a dummy address; we will add an address in the next activity. You can do this by casting the document to dynamic and then to a transaction, using `Newtonsoft` to turn it into a string, and then adding it as a `StringContent`. Refer to the following screenshot:

You have a function triggered by new transactions.

This function is more powerful than it initially seems. It is driven by an event, risen by an application that shares no code with it whatsoever. It doesn't need the developer to deploy or create a complex queue management application to achieve it, either; it simply uses built-in functionality. You can add many different functions, all triggered by this same event, and your first application will never have to change. You can keep adding features that are totally independent of one another.

Functions have a fairly limited set of connectors built in when compared to Logic Apps which encourages you to decouple the connection mechanism into a Logic App, and an Azure Function for the complex processing. Luckily, that's very easy, because both are triggered by HTTP requests.

Triggering an Azure Logic App from an Azure Function

Having captured an event with an Azure Function, we want to integrate with another system that doesn't have an Azure Functions connector. You will need the Azure Function from the first example, to ensure our system works correctly. Let's begin by implementing the following steps:

1. Open the Azure portal and search for the precise phrase Logic App in the marketplace. Create a new Logic App.
2. Use the resource group you created earlier. There's no need to switch on log analytics; choose the same location that you use for the rest of your services.
3. Once the Logic App is deployed, find it through a search. The Logic Apps designer should open automatically; if it doesn't, click on **Overview**, and **Edit**.
4. Click when an HTTP request is received under common triggers. Refer to the following screenshot:

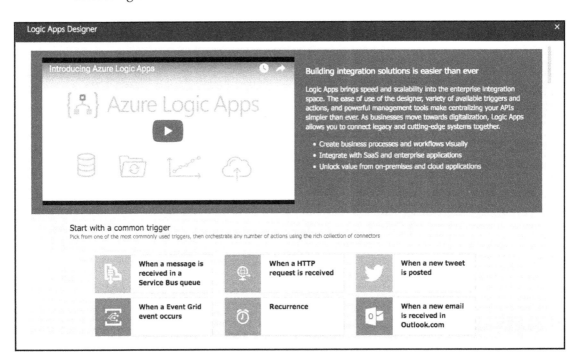

5. You should now have a Logic App that looks something like the screenshot. Save the Logic App, and copy and paste the URL that appears into the address that your function calls.

6. You can test this by clicking **Run** on the **Logic Apps Designer** and then adding a transaction to the Cosmos DB. It may take a little while (the reporting is quite slow), but your HTTP request box should get a green tick. This shows that a run has been successfully triggered:

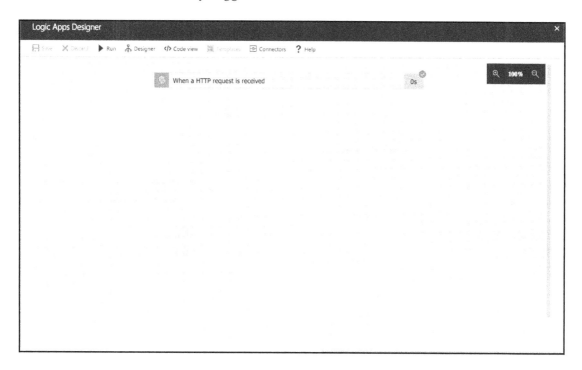

You have triggered a Logic App using a Cosmos DB transaction.

Now that the Cosmos DB event has triggered a Logic App, there's a whole host of things that you can do. Logic Apps are really a massive box of connectors to all sorts of different services. Here are a few examples:

> Find out more about connectors, including how to write your own for others to use, at https://docs.microsoft.com/en-gb/connectors/.

Power BI is a powerful business intelligence tool. Built to seem familiar to both those who come from an Excel background and those who write R, it is very powerful, and very easy to use. When you take a look around the Logic Apps interface in the example later, you'll see its connector. You can create live-updating graphs and reports for your analysts as new transactions come in, and you can embed those charts into a web page for your customer to view directly. Power BI comes with lots of built-in charts and drilldowns. For example, if you submit data with country information, it will immediately put it on a world map and allow the viewer to drill down to the country level.

 You can learn more about Power BI at `https://powerbi.microsoft.com/en-us/`.

Azure Data Lake is Microsoft's premier Hadoop filesystem-based service. It splits files across hundreds of machines, ready for massively parallelized processing jobs initiated by Azure Data Lake Analytics. It's possible to build an architecture utilizing Azure Functions, pushing data into the Azure Data Lake and using Azure Data Lake Analytics to process huge datasets. Alone, Azure Functions will struggle to complete massive processing jobs, due to their relatively short timeout and their inability to parallelize processing massively on a single large file. U-SQL, the language that Azure Data Lake Analytics is written in, compiles into C++ programs on different machines that handle their own threading and read simultaneously from a large file. It's a great way to get data into a state fit for machine learning or further analysis.

 You can find out more about Azure Data Lake at `https://azure.microsoft.com/en-in/solutions/data-lake/`.

Azure also offers a series of cognitive APIs, which are pre-canned machine learning services. It's relatively straightforward to plug your own ML algorithms in, through either Azure Machine Learning Studio or an HTTP request. The cognitive APIs offer features such as translation (very useful for saving the effort of retraining your machine learning algorithm when expanding to a new country), sentiment analysis on both facial images and text (useful for triaging customer complaints, for example), and keyword analysis (useful for the categorization of requests). There is also LUIS, which is Microsoft's chatbot building service.

 Learn more about cognitive services at `https://azure.microsoft.com/en-gb/services/cognitive-services/`.

Sending a Reminder Email

In this section, we'll check the weather forecast and send our user an email, reminding them to save for a rainy day. We want to encourage good savings behavior in our users with innovative notifications. And to ensure that it works correctly, we'll need the Azure Logic App from the second example. Let begin by implementing the following steps:

1. Open your Logic App in the portal and click on **Edit**. The **Logic Apps Designer** will be shown.
2. Check that you are in designer view, not code view.
3. Click on the + icon below your HTTP request trigger. Click on **Add an action**. Search for `Weather` in the search box, and select **Get the forecast for tomorrow**.
4. Choose your **Location** and whichever **Units** you are comfortable with. We will be using percentages, so it doesn't matter whether you use the **Metric** or **Imperial System**. We could query our user database for their location.
5. Click the + button below your weather box, and then click **Add a condition**.
6. Place your cursor inside of the left-hand box and search for `Rain Chance` in the **Dynamic content** box that appears. Refer to the following screenshot:

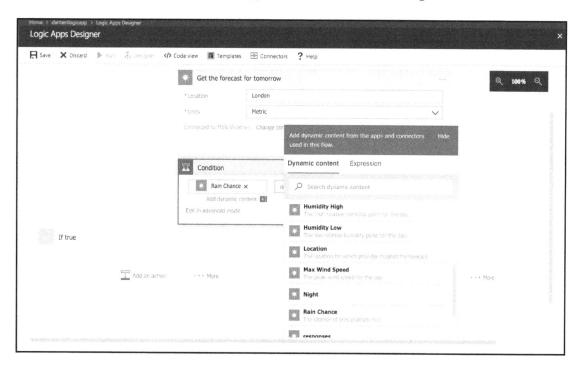

7. Set the condition to **Greater than**, and enter `0.9` in the right-hand box. This will trigger if the chance of rain tomorrow is greater than 90 percent.

8. Your Logic App will now display paths for the true and false conditions.

> There are lots of different logical constructs in Logic Apps, but one thing to remember is this: if you find yourself using a massive `switch` statement, or logic-forking more than a couple of times, then you need to split your Logic App up. It's important that your logic app stays simple, you can split complex ones up into either more logic apps or Azure Functions. The reason for this is that they were originally designed to be relatively simple, and they quickly become unmanageable once they grow beyond a few true/false branches.

9. Add an action to the **True fork** and search for email.

10. There are a lot of connectors; the main ones are Gmail and Outlook. If you select **Send an email**, the email provider will ask you to sign in. If you already have an account with one of them, then sign-in to it. If you don't have one sign up for a free account with one of them.

11. Set the **To** field to an email address that you have access to. Set the **Subject** to **Save for a rainy day!**

12. In the body of the email, you can add some dynamic content. It'd be great if we could use content from our request in the same way that we used the data from the weather forecast, and luckily, we can. Click on the HTTP request trigger, and click **Generate schema** from example payload. Copy and paste a transaction payload from **Postman**.

13. Click in the body of the email and search for amount in your **Dynamic content** menu. Now that there's a schema, we can use this data. Insert it. Write a message similar to the one in the following screenshot:

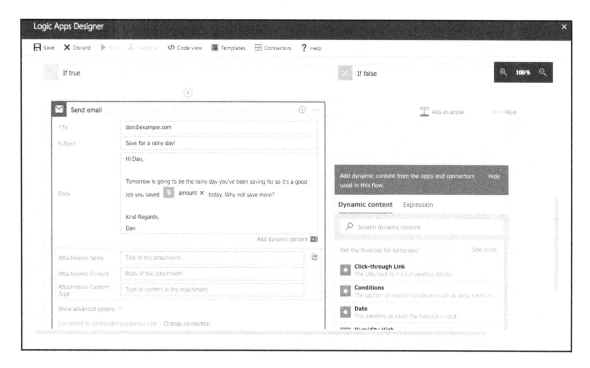

This is a tricky Logic App to test, unless you live somewhere very rainy! So, let's cheat and set the probability of rain forecasted to be higher than to 0. Then, send another transaction from Postman.

You have successfully created a Logic App with logical conditions, schema, and dynamic content, and you have sent an email based on live weather conditions.

Integrating Legacy Applications

If you are operating on a totally greenfield project, everything that we have discussed so far will work perfectly. The full variety of SaaS, PaaS, and IaaS integrations means that your serverless code will happily operate with any set of requirements. Where things tend to get tricky is legacy systems. Whether they are written in a programming language that is no longer supported inside your firm, are monolithic and difficult to extend, or are completely black box, these applications do tend to perform vital business functions and therefore cannot be left out in the cold. If there is an API then integration is straightforward, but sadly there often isn't one. Either a gargantuan development effort needs to be made to replace them or they need to be integrated into the new architecture.

Serverless can come to the rescue for most cases, although there will always be some applications written so uniquely that it's impossible to help them.

First, we'll look at the easiest way that serverless can help. If your app has an API, you can just call it directly; but if there's a lot of development going on with this application, then you may end up replicating a lot of the API calls. If you have an OpenAPI definition, then you can create a custom connector for Logic Apps (and a few other Microsoft services) that allows other developers to use it, as you have been using the Gmail connector (and so on) in Logic Apps.

 Learn more about creating custom connectors at `https://docs.microsoft.com/en-us/connectors/custom-connectors/create-logic-apps-connector`.

Secondly, if your application has code that you can change (in other words, if it is open source or written internally), then you can simply add HTTP requests that trigger serverless functions. This will effectively allow you to create events when certain methods are triggered.

Triggering a Function from a Legacy Application

In this section, we'll trigger an Azure Function from a console application. We'll integrate an existing command-line application with our new cloud architecture. To ensure it works correctly, you'll need to have the code repository downloaded. Let's begin by implementing the following steps:

1. Open the project called `PersonalFinanceCLIApp` and take a look around.

This application is a command-line application that allows a user to submit a transaction, save it into a CSV, and then produce some stats about the transactions that have been logged with the app. This is obviously a very simple example of a legacy application, written in C# so that students are able to edit it, but the principles of what we will do apply to any general-purpose programming language with access to network interfaces.

Refer to the following screenshot:

Refer to the complete code placed at `Code/Serverless-Architectures-with-Azure/Lesson 3/PersonalFinanceCLIApp/Program.cs`. Navigate to `https://goo.gl/q79fPe` to access the code.

2. Add an `HttpClient` and your API key as static variables.

 Get your API key by going to your function in the portal and clicking on the **Keys** tab.

Refer to the following screenshot:

 Refer to the complete code placed at `Code/Serverless-Architectures-with-Azure/Lesson 3/PersonalFinanceCLIApp/PersonalFinanceCLIApp.csproj`. Navigate to `https://goo.gl/E88BMn` to access the code.

3. Create an async static function called `BackupTransaction` that takes a `transaction` object. In the function, copy and paste the code from our serverless client POST action. Refer to the following screenshot:

4. Make a call to `BackupTransactions` and pass the transaction into it.
5. Run the CLI app; it should be just as responsive as it was previously, because the asynchronous code is executing on a separate thread.

You have successfully written an application that backs transactions up to the Cosmos DB.

Thirdly, if you have a fairly well-architected application written in a programming language that your development team can cope with, then you can progressively shift functionality to serverless functions without breaking the application. This allows you to split the work up to replace the application entirely, and, once you have this data flowing through serverless functions, you can start extending this application into the rest of your serverless architecture.

This functionality will then be available for other services to use, which is particularly useful for intensive, business-specific calculations. It will also scale infinitely, allowing you to free up computing power from your client machines (this is very useful for code running on old servers, and so on).

Moving Functionality from a Legacy Application to an Azure Function

In this section, we'll calculate the interesting facts about the users' transactions in an Azure Function. We'll offload intensive processing from a legacy application to a serverless function. To ensure it works correctly, we'll need to have the code repository downloaded. Let's begin by implementing the following steps:

1. Create a new `HttpTriggered` function called `CalculateTransactionsInformation`. Set the access rights to `Anonymous`.

2. Delete everything in the `Run` function template. Refer to the following screenshot:

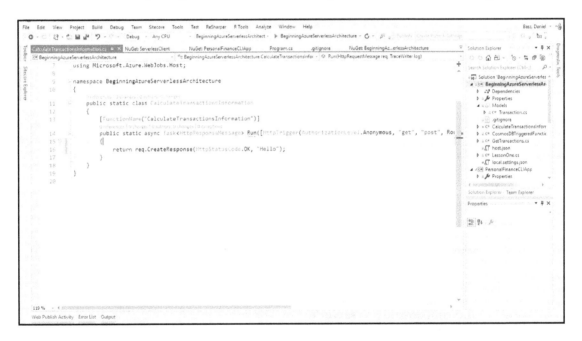

Refer to the complete code placed at `Code/Serverless-Architectures-with-Azure/Lesson 3/BeginningAzureServerlessArchitecture/CalculateTransactionsInformation.cs`.
Navigate to `https://goo.gl/WHTjEY` to access the code.

3. Deserialize the content of the message into a list of transactions; you can copy some of the code from `LessonOne.cs`. Refer to the following screenshot:

```
using Microsoft.Azure.WebJobs.Host;
using Newtonsoft.Json;

namespace BeginningAzureServerlessArchitecture
{
    public static class CalculateTransactionsInformation
    {
        [FunctionName("CalculateTransactionsInformation")]
        public static async Task<HttpResponseMessage> Run([HttpTrigger(AuthorizationLevel.Anonymous, "get", "post", Route = null
        {
            var message = req.Content.ReadAsStringAsync().Result;

            List<Transaction> transactions = new List<Transaction>();

            try
            {
                transactions.AddRange(JsonConvert.DeserializeObject<List<Transaction>>(message));
            }
            catch (Exception e)
            {
                return req.CreateErrorResponse(HttpStatusCode.BadRequest, "The request did not match the required schema");
            }

            return req.CreateResponse(HttpStatusCode.OK, "Hello");
        }
    }
}
```

 Refer to the complete code placed at `Code/Serverless-Architectures-with-Azure/Lesson 3/BeginningAzureServerlessArchitecture/LessonOne.cs`. Navigate to `https://goo.gl/o5zW1x` to access the code.

4. Cut and paste the LINQ statements from the CLI app. Refer to the following screenshot:

```csharp
ng Microsoft.Azure.WebJobs.Host;
ng Newtonsoft.Json;

espace BeginningAzureServerlessArchitecture

public static class CalculateTransactionsInformation
{
    [FunctionName("CalculateTransactionsInformation")]
    public static async Task<HttpResponseMessage> Run([HttpTrigger(AuthorizationLevel.Anonymous, "get", "post", Route = nul
    {
        var message = req.Content.ReadAsStringAsync().Result;

        List<Transaction> transactions = new List<Transaction>();
        try
        {
            transactions.AddRange(JsonConvert.DeserializeObject<List<Transaction>>(message));
        }
        catch (Exception e)
        {
            return req.CreateErrorResponse(HttpStatusCode.BadRequest, "The request did not match the required schema");
        }

        return req.CreateResponse(HttpStatusCode.OK, "Hello");
    }
}
```

 Refer to the complete code placed at `Code/Serverless-Architectures-with-Azure/Lesson 3/BeginningAzureServerlessArchitecture/CalculateTransactionsInformation.cs`.
Navigate to `https://goo.gl/WHTjEY` to access the code.

5. Let's add a model to make it easier to transfer the results between the functions. Create a model called `TransactionsInformationModel` with three decimal properties: `TotalTransactionsAmount`, `MeanTransactionAmount`, and `LargestTransactionAmount`. Refer to the following screenshot:

Refer to the complete code placed at `Code/Serverless-Architectures-with-Azure/Lesson 3/BeginningAzureServerlessArchitecture/Models/Transactions InformationModel.cs`.
Navigate to `https://goo.gl/3UCjeg` to access the code.

6. Now return an instance of the `TransactionsInformationModel` in the response content. Refer to the following screenshot:

```csharp
try
{
    transactions.AddRange(JsonConvert.DeserializeObject<List<Transaction>>(message));
}
catch (Exception e)
{
    return req.CreateErrorResponse(HttpStatusCode.BadRequest, "The request did not match the required schema");
}

var totalTransactions = transactions.Sum(t => t.Amount);
var meanTransactionSize = transactions.Average(t => t.Amount);
var largestTransactionAmount = transactions.Max(t => t.Amount);

var transactionsInformation = new TransactionsInformationModel
{
    TotalTransactionsAmount = totalTransactions,
    MeanTransactionAmount = meanTransactionSize,
    LargestTransactionAmount = largestTransactionAmount
};

var jsonTransactionsInformation = JsonConvert.SerializeObject(transactionsInformation);

return req.CreateResponse(HttpStatusCode.OK, jsonTransactionsInformation);
```

Refer to the complete code placed at `Code/Serverless-Architectures-with-Azure/Lesson 3/BeginningAzureServerlessArchitecture/CalculateTransactionsInformation.cs`.

Navigate to `https://goo.gl/7BjuhC` to access the code.

7. Return to the console application, in `Program.cs`. Add another function that takes a list of transactions and returns a `TransactionsInformationModel` called `CalculateTransactionInformation`. Refer to the following screenshot:

If Intellisense has an issue with this, click **Build** on the Function App project. Serialize the transactions into a string content, with code similar to before. There's no point in making this asynchronous, because the application depends on showing this before the message asking the user whether they want to add another transaction. So, add a `.Result` on to the end of every asynchronous method. Deserialize the response into the `TransactionInformationModel`.

Refer to the complete code placed at `Code/Serverless-Architectures-with-Azure/Lesson 3/PersonalFinanceCLIApp/Program.cs`.
Navigate to `https://goo.gl/PqcU8u` to access the code.

8. Add a method call where the LINQ statements were, pass the result into `var`, and change the references in the `Console.logs` to point to the corresponding properties on that object. Refer to the following screenshot:

9. Deploy your function to Azure and copy and paste the address of it into the `HttpRequest`.

10. Test the app.

Statistical calculations have shifted from one application to a serverless function.

What if you either don't have access to the source code, or it is so delicate that the previous approaches are unfathomable? Well, another method for serverless integration is to target the database directly. Whether it's an application brought in or a delicate, internal application, applications will tend to have their very own databases, likely on-premises rather than cloud-based. Microsoft has a product called the **On-premises data gateway** that allows you to connect serverless functions to On-premises PostgreSQL, MySQL, Oracle, SQL, and Teradata databases, as well as MQ and BizTalk servers. You can then trigger serverless functions when records are added to some of these databases or messages are added to MQ. This product is relatively easy to set up, but obviously, setting up a miniature data center for you to try this out in the book would be a bit lengthy, so we won't be doing it.

Find out how to set up the On-premises data gateway at `https://docs.microsoft.com/en-us/azure/logic-apps/logic-apps-gateway-connection`.

Activity: Extending Your Serverless Application

Prerequisites

You will need previous functions from end-of-chapter activities.

Scenario

Extending an application by combining data sources together.

Aim

Combine your transactions and users together to identify which users made transactions, and extend your application.

Steps for Completion

1. Delete everything from your `transactions` collection. Add a property to your transaction that matches the unique identifier from the users collection.
2. Change your Logic App so that it will look up an email address from the users collection, using the ID from the transaction that triggered the Logic App. Use this email address as the address you send the notification to. Add more details from the user record to the email to personalize it, such as their name or gender.
3. Add login functionality with a password, and prevent anyone from submitting transactions directly to the serverless API without the correct username and password.
4. Create a new client application for the serverless backend in a language or framework of your choice.

You have an application sending customized emails to users, extended with user logins.

Refer to the complete code placed at `Code/Serverless-Architectureswith-Azure/Lesson 3/BeginningAzureServerlessArchitecture/Models/`.

Before the transactions have taken place:

- `User.cs`: Go to `https://goo.gl/bFjWNv` to access the code
- `Transaction.cs`: Go to `https://goo.gl/31h6SN` to access the code
- `GetUsers.cs`: Go to `https://goo.gl/i6qxVA` to access the code

After the transactions have taken place:

- `PostUsers.cs`: Go to `https://goo.gl/WqZ4p5` to access the code
- `PostTransactions.cs`: Go to `https://goo.gl/J4XuZd` to access the code

Summary

In this chapter, you've covered techniques for building greenfield serverless architectures (where you can exploit the full potential of serverless) and techniques for integrating existing applications. You now know how to connect to a wide variety of services through Logic Apps, a simple-to-use serverless product. You know several approaches for integrating your existing applications into a serverless architecture, from creating a custom API connector to adding event triggering on to an existing database.

In this book, you have started with an introduction to Azure Functions. Here you analyzed the real benefits of Serverless Computing and the technical basis of Azure Functions. Once your Azure Function was deployed, you integrated it with other Azure Services and logged with Application Insights.

Then, you secured the server with API Keys. Lastly, you implemented a Greenfield Serverless Application and integrated a legacy application with Serverless Architecture.

This solid base allows you to build your own serverless solutions to meet any future requirement.

Other Books You May Enjoy

If you enjoyed this book, you may be interested in these other books by Packt:

Learning Azure Functions
Manisha Yadav, Mitesh Soni

ISBN: 978-1-78712-293-2

- Understand the folder structure of a function and the purposes of the files
- Deploy a function and test it
- Explore the common triggers that are used to activate a function
- Discover how bindings can be used to output the results of a function
- Build a dll that has functionality that can be leveraged by a function
- Chain functions to allow the invocation of one function from another
- Understand how to monitor the health of your functions

Azure Serverless Computing Cookbook
Praveen Kumar Sreeram

ISBN: 978-1-78839-082-8

- Develop different event-based handlers supported by serverless architecture supported by Microsoft Cloud Platform – Azure
- Integrate Azure Functions with different Azure Services to develop Enterprise-level applications
- Get to know the best practices in organizing and refactoring the code within the Azure Functions
- Test, troubleshoot, and monitor the Azure Functions to deliver high-quality, reliable, and robust cloud-centric applications
- Automate mundane tasks at various levels right from development to deployment and maintenance
- Learn how to develop stateful serverless applications and also self-healing jobs using DurableFunctions

Leave a review - let other readers know what you think

Please share your thoughts on this book with others by leaving a review on the site that you bought it from. If you purchased the book from Amazon, please leave us an honest review on this book's Amazon page. This is vital so that other potential readers can see and use your unbiased opinion to make purchasing decisions, we can understand what our customers think about our products, and our authors can see your feedback on the title that they have worked with Packt to create. It will only take a few minutes of your time, but is valuable to other potential customers, our authors, and Packt. Thank you!

Index